Dear Gravity

Books by Gregory Djanikian

The Man in the Middle
Falling Deeply into America
About Distance
Years Later
So I Will Till the Ground
Dear Gravity

Dear Gravity

Poems by Gregory Djanikian

To Janet,

with best
wishes,

Gregory
Djanikian

Carnegie Mellon University Press
Pittsburgh 2014

ACKNOWLEDGMENTS

Grateful acknowledgment is made to the editors of the magazines in which some of these poems first appeared:

Alhambra Poetry Calendar 2010: "Beginnings"; *Alhambra Poetry Calendar 2011*: "Swimming at Agami Beach"; *The American Poetry Review*: "Pre-Induction Physical"; *The American Scholar*: "Something to Think About"; *Boulevard*: "Against the Symbolism of Small Losses," "Animal Deaths," "Outside the Window in July," "Something Else," "Song of Imponderables," "The Book of Love"; *ConnotationPress.com*: "Arizona Wind," "Conversation with Landscape," "My Uncle's Eye," "Sailing to Lebanon," "The Groove"; *The Cortland Review*: "Anger," "Arizona Ranch," "Free Love," "Rural Accident"; *The Iowa Review*: "High School Lesson"; *Miramar*: "Cutlass Supreme," "Night Traveling in Northern Vermont," "Something Changing"; *New Ohio Review*: "Piano Lesson," "Superman at 95"; *One Trick Pony*: "Lost Poems"; *Per Contra*: "On a Nature Walk in the Southwest," "One Afternoon"; *Poetry*: "First Efforts," "Mind | Body"; *Poetry Northwest*: "Arc Welding on Night Shift," "Immigration Test," "Poem," "The Feel of Feeling It"; *Smartish Pace*: "First Winter in America"; *The Southern Review*: "Anxiety of Influence," "Violence"; *Superstition Review*: "Love Poem with Crowbar," "Questions for a Late Night"; *Tar River Poetry Review*: "The Future As a Notion of Momentary Pleasures," "Writer's Block"; *TriQuarterly*: "Talking to Myself in the Shower"; *XConnect*: "Embarrassment," "Why I Have the Radio On"; "Talking to Myself in the Shower" appeared in the anthology of poems, *Seriously Funny: Poems About Love, Death, Religion, Art, Politics, Sex, and Everything Else*, edited by Barbara Hamby and David Kirby (University of Georgia Press, 2010). "Violence" appeared as a featured poem on *Poetry Daily*. "First Winter in America" appeared as a featured poem on *Verse Daily*.

My thanks to the Corporation of Yaddo for two residencies during which some of these poems were written. Thanks also to Stephen Dunn for his helpful suggestions that improved many of the poems, to Phil Sandick for pointing me to the title, and to my wife, Alysa Bennett, for her keen advice in bringing the book to fruition.

Book design by Lou Lamanna

Library of Congress Control Number 2013937108
ISBN 978-0-88748-578-7

for my sister, Tania

CONTENTS

I

II

III

I

Violence

Sometimes it can't be avoided
even though you might decline
the invitation to step outside—
sometimes you *are* outside

maybe in the repose of your garden
among rose petal and fern, but the whole
unvarnished spectacle of do
before you're done unto unfolding
as spider devours beetle, beetle, aphid,
and the cat red in the tooth and claw.

No need to bring up bombs bursting
in synch or the rockets' red glare
or every laser fescue pointing out
all that's erasable, goodbye goodbye.

It's among school children now,
maybe even in your neighbor's house,
eating ravenously at his table,
agreeing with everything he says.

Inside, your daughter is locking
all the basement windows, your son
is drawing a truth machine to zap
the bad from the good, and when
your wife comes home to tell you
of a small injustice she's endured,
the arrow of your steely retribution
thwunks into a soft, imagined heart.

No one immune here, no one
merely a small flash in the pan:
everything hugely combustible.

In the garden, you're dead-heading
lilies, the petals spiraling down

like crushed wings, and your fingers,
steeped in pulp, are turning yellow,
orange, incarnadine, damage
creating its own aesthetic,
painting itself on your skin.

And if anyone asked you now
you'd confess you're damage too,
you're for wreckage of heart and bone
wrenching out the smallest penance.
Above you, purple bruising the edges
of the sky. Even the heavens.

In another moment, someone
might come looking for you,
touch you on the shoulder
and you'd flame up.

Nothing seems so improbable
as the world of a few minutes ago.

Here's the night full of stars.
Behind each one, the darkness
you can never see.

Arc Welding on Night Shift

We were lighting up the factory,
the hot-white current
striking through wire and steel.

"I'm a hooded assassin," Tubbsy said laughing,
bending over and pulling the trigger.

Some of us were sheathed in thick denim,
some in heavy leather, the sparks
burning small craters into our gloves.

If we weren't careful with our aim
we could run wire clear through our palms.
If we raised our hoods too soon,
we would tear all night from the blindness.

We were doing piecework, welding
gussets to tubing, rods to plates,
but who knew what we were making,
how it was adding up, where it was going.

We were trying to keep our verticals true,
one streak of steel melting into another
and cooling into such a ribbed hardness

it was beautiful, Willis said,
pulling his hood off,
running his fingers softly
along the spine of a bead,

something so incidental to all
our fire and arc it took us by surprise
to see it being touched

not knowing exactly
what it was about, only
that it was among us now,

coming and going all night
without regard of who we were,
where it was taking hold.

THE INVENTION OF DEATH

Nothing was so mysterious
as your body coming to a close,
the winches of your arms and legs
slackening, your mouth loosened.

You were lying under a white coverlet
as if under a field of snow.

Something was beginning to drift
like the sound of a train in the distance
under the color of sky.

It was difficult to think
that train is for you, not me
but it was almost easy too.

The birds outside the window
were breaking the glassiness of the morning,
the merciful were disguised
as women in white gowns.

You opened your eyes and asked
what I would remember of you
and I couldn't help but think *this*

you in a field of snow
and the train waiting by a platform
and the invention of death
twittering outside with feathers.

If language hadn't failed me then
and I remembered speaking.

If silence hadn't entered and sat down
like a fat dark uncle on your bed
and begun stroking your hand.

Song of Imponderables

My father was thin and his bones were quiet,
the bed was a raft in the waves of night.

My father was quiet and the night was shallow,
the moon was the only shape in the sky.

There were no stars to steer a course,
there was no bell to toll the hour.

My father was still, and his face was open,
the body rising and falling in a circle.

The wind was a solitude among small reeds.
The water turned on a hinge of silence.

There were no stars to steer a course,
no bell to toll the hour.

My father lay in the shape of his sleep,
and the sleep of his body was undisturbed.

The moon was a circle closing its eye.
The dark was unfolding its many hands.

Rural Accident

What would you do on a night
with no moon in the starless sky

and the summery grass wet
and colder than summer,

and a motorcycle suddenly visible
in your headlights, crumpled halfway

up a field, a helmet lying
by the side of the road

and a voice from the ditch by that road
calling *help me* to whom else but you

and you with no phone
and no stomach for such things

aiming your headlights on the body
the leg bent severely

the bone sticking out, the face
sixteen, unmarked, surprised

to be where it is or to watch you
walking awkwardly toward him

and what do you do when there's
no needle or morphine

you like a bad angel hoping
for some nerve of his to snap

or a deeper sleep to come
and lift the burden of responsibility

I'll get help, you say, throwing
your sweater over him, touching his hair

remembering the house with lights
shining a couple of miles away

and what if it were your son
lying crumpled in the ditch

and crying out sharply
from the middle of nowhere

what would you *not* do to lug him
into your car, jutting bones and all

no matter how loudly he howled
or how the howling knifed at your gut

but all you're doing now
is turning away

leaving him in the wet grass
with his crushed voice

without someone to stand
over him and spread his hands

on everything broken
someone like you

getting into your car
speeding toward the distant lights

through every dangerous curve
as if your recklessness were a kind of mercy

as if you were doing all you could
to ward off the darkness

the faster you drove,
the further you left him behind.

SUPERMAN AT 95

It was never a question of age, finally.
Time for him had always moved
too slowly, wasn't he faster than time,
outrunning it whenever he wished?
Even now, he could hear the sound
of every second before it clicked.

Oh, he was powerful enough,
still wildly aerodynamic, able
to leap imagination itself.

But he'd grown weary of it all,
the adoring looks, the caped crusading
in the name of righteousness and truth:
hadn't it frayed a little, lost
its gleam through the turbulent years?

Nothing had changed really,
annihilation, ruin, the horsemen
of every apocalypse still riding through
like bad cops and pestilence,
knowing where everyone lived.

And his own life, emptier now
with so many friends gone
or on the way, Jimmy, Lois,
doddering in their last stages
in a metropolis of fear.

Even his shadow-self had had to die,
mild-mannered to the end, grown
stooped, with failing eyesight.
Who would he be tomorrow?
Car salesman? Auto mechanic?
It was all greasepaint and mirrors,
so many cheap parlor tricks
everyone seemed fooled by.

What he wanted more and more
was pouring himself a drink,
turning the TV up like everyone else,
some canned laughter for the road—
and always, there was too much road,
too many voices buzzing in his ear, asking him
for liberty, for justice, things that required
compromises, disappointments.

Frankly, he'd always been better
at disasters, a couple of earthquakes
to attend to, some small-time hoods.
And a beautiful woman on his arm
with a bird's-eye view of the earth
that could still astound.

Sometimes he found himself lying back,
scanning the night sky without X-ray eyes,
without the hair-trigger hearing.

He liked not knowing what would come next,
feeling his head against the ground,
his palms cool on the moist grass,
being able to see only as far
as the darkness would allow.

THE FEEL OF FEELING IT

> *When there is none to heal it,*
> *Nor numbèd sense to steel it . . .*
> —Keats

Everyone's asleep: the house
is breathing deeply, lucky house.

Your eyes: jags of sensation,
unlucky, insomniac,

the living room a forest of snags
around the lake you wish was there.

Your mind says *boredom, a little sleep*
Your body says *sleep, a little death*

If you could walk out of yourself
and be the thin gray shadow

sliding quickly
over all the surfaces, goodbye!

No rest, no waking slow,
just the feel of feeling it,

the wading through,
thick world without end.

Soon the sun: messenger
with news you've already read.

And the others waking easily
with all their *good mornings,*

such strange companions now
arriving in another language.

ANGER

Wherever there's a raucousness of birds,
    there may be someone below
almost wishing to pitch stones
  at wing and beak,

the mind sometimes
    of two minds, combative,
propitiatory, arrows
  pointing in unlike directions.

A man sitting in a park by himself
    talking too loudly
as if to an antagonist
  might startle himself with so much rancor

his body will pull back, his words
    disarm themselves into a hum.
Some moments require a gentling
  of heart, an exhalation,

from the French, *vent*, for wind,
    to pour out, to issue forth
after the first sharp grip
  of compression.

To pick up a knife is often
    to make too much of a point.
To cock the hammer of a gun is to give
  the finger more license than it deserves.

All those birds that might be singing
    in spite of anyone's ill will.
When happiness comes, it, too, comes
  with a mouth, as an utterance, spills.

QUESTIONS FOR A LATE NIGHT

And what if the soldiers came
shouting and clattering, pulling you
out of your house for the journey
which had no clear destination

What if the road you had to follow
looking for fruit trees, spring water
had to be imagined each morning
no jacarandas offering you shade
the deserts wafting you
like a husk in the simoom

What if the granaries were leveled, the rivers dry
young girls bruised in the thighs
the birdlike men without feet

What would the darkness bring you
wolf howls, hoof beats
sticking you like needles
if all you wanted of it
was a place to enter, disguised
from the smallest reflection

What if there were no night
the heavens dismantled, the earth
lit by a hundred suns

What if you were the perpetual witness
walking without sleep
where everyone desired it
and no one dared close his eyes

What could you say
to remember the sound of heartbreak
In what place would you touch your body
to feel your body touching you back

PRE-INDUCTION PHYSICAL

Philadelphia, 1971

We were being lobbed, mortared,
thrown into the explosions
of a new decade, called up,
dressed down, asked who we were,
what were we willing to give.

We were a democracy of numbers,
the best bodies of our generation stripped down
to briefs and jockeys, bending over,
moving to doctors' orders, station
to station to eye charts, ear scans,
psycho-troubles behind the curtained stalls.

It was Vietnam, nine thousand miles away,
but it was everywhere, in all our faces.

Outside, marches, flag-burnings, guerilla
theater in the warfare parks, massacres wounding
the body common at My Lai, Kent State,

and we were standing shoulder to shoulder,
the freaks and the straights, the queers
and the love-it-or-leave-it apostles,
smelling disinfectant along the white-tiled walls,
the fluorescence humming
like something pitched to go off.

"Legally blind in Pennsylvania,"
someone was proving with his thick lenses,
and someone else was waving his X-rays
like a glossy passport, the accident,
the pins in his tibia, all of us
hating him, his good luck.

Some of us were already burning,
thermally damaged, Joey dowsing his foot
with boiling water the night before,
Frank stubbing out cigarettes on his arm,
fire wherever we turned, self-immolations,
Buddhists, Quakers, Norman Morrison
at the Pentagon, Thich Quang Duc
kerosened in Saigon, and the napalm fighters
diving down to the firework trenches.

We were looking at each other
trying to measure ourselves by the next in line
and a sergeant was asking the gangliest kid
"You want in or out?" and no one
knew how to answer it, the calibrations,
the minefields involved, what anyone said
maybe coming back like a guided missile
leveling the ground we teetered on.

Someone was being led away,
no draft card, no excuses, someone
was sitting teary-eyed in the corner
and maybe all of us were thinking *that's not me*
or wishing it was, without shame.

We were lost to the future,
leaving a decade behind us,
the red smear of assassinations,
the flower children junked up,
Woodstock, Altamont, the smell
of grass and gunpowder newly
inseparable, Maharishi and Manson
both let loose on the flesh of the world.

It was Vietnam, Vietnam,
the word echoing along the skin
and America lay in every blister

and rash on the body, every wound
calling out for a mystery to heal it,
and the soul famishing
in its cage of bones

and we were shuffling in single file
as if underwater, as if years might pass
before any sound could reach us,
the information garbled when it might come,
1-A, 1-Y, 4-F, letters, numbers sometimes
transposed in our heads, crisscrossing
like F-4 Phantoms over the sniper trees.

Do you want to stay in or out?
That was the question, hanging
on a hook behind every face,
written invisibly in the veins of our arms,
lip-synched in every cubicle,

and we were 18, 21, thinking
of what it took to aim between the eyes,
to feel, halfway naked as we were,
something hard and invisible entering the body
and the body unfolding.

We were standing together and alone,
we were brothers and never brothers
about to swerve, the luckier of us
only for a while or maybe hardly at all,
some others, forever and deeply,

and someone was raising his fist in jubilation
and another already had the eyes of the remorseful
and one of us was shaking his head *no no*
and another was speaking to his hands

and we were at the end of the line now
putting our clothes back on and hiding the body,
we were walking out the door and seeing
the orange sun slowly falling like a giant flare,
flare of promise and desire we faintly remembered
from our past lives of just this morning,
radiance we couldn't look at for too long
for fear of suddenly believing it.

II

SWIMMING AT AGAMI BEACH

Alexandria, 1955

The waves were crashing like wild horses,
no one could ride them.

I stood in the shallows
feeling their power to startle me away
or hold me spellbound.

The horses were dark and fierce,
galloping toward me,
kicking their forelegs and hooves.

There was salt in my mouth,
the sand was in every crevice,
I was dreaming of the end of world.

I wanted to fall through their sound
where I would be new to it,
every molecule of water, every
kiss of sand against my skin.

I stood watching them
frothing and unreined
as if in a dream that felt so true
it was neither phantom nor wish,

as if there were nothing left to do
but hold out my hand
and walk out among them.

My Uncle's Eye

Alexandria, 1954

It had happened on a small Cairo street,
the shops smelling of dark leather,
the hookah parlors spilling out
onto the crowded sidewalk.

It had been a fight, someone
throwing a bottle at my uncle's face,
the slivers lodging deep.

I stared hard at that blind watery sheen.
I thought my uncle must live
a shadow life, imagining with one eye
what the other couldn't see.

I walked one day through the house
with my hand over half my face,
bumping into things, swiveling my head.

"Silly boy," my grandmother said,
knitting quietly in her armchair,
"what's to become of you?"

"Loony brain," my sister warbled,
twirling gauzily away like a ballerina.

But I knew my uncle would be arriving for a visit,
driving from Cairo on the long desert road,
and he would be making time,
measuring speeds.

And I was practicing how to move
the way he moved, skimming along
hazy edges, judging distances
by inkling, relying on some part
of the tangible world

without knowing exactly
what to hold on to,
what to let go.

SAILING TO LEBANON

1957, after the Suez War

We were steaming northward, leaving
Alexandria behind us, the white city
receding, floating at the edge of the sea.

My sister and I were singing together,
"Day-ay-ay O . . . me wan' go home,"
something we'd heard on the radio
though we didn't know where home was
or if we'd ever see Stanley Bay again,
the minarets, the tram cars at Ramleh Station.

We wanted to be Harry Belafonte on a record,
we wanted to be in America
where everything might last for some time.

Our parents were talking in whispers.
Clouds were passing across the sun.
It was almost evening, we had never seen
the horizon as far away as it was.

In our small cabin with the porthole open
we could hear the sound of the ocean
lapping at the ship's side,
we were smelling the odor
of salt, iron, rust.

In a few days, we would be in Bhamdoun,
Dhour El Choueir, mountain towns
where we could stay a few weeks
looking for further passage.

Everything seemed on a rise and fall,
the sea was growing thicker.

Sometimes the fog was so heavy
the ship's horn would sound
and we'd be startled into laughter.

"It's the old man snoring," I'd say,
and we'd think of someone so fast asleep
he wakes up years later in a different country,
walking in a daze, singing
all the songs he's never known.

First Winter in America

I walked out into the January blizzard,
my breath froze into small clouds,
and ice was hanging from the trees.

The dunes were dreamy animals,
I heard shovels striking music.

White eyelashes, white mittens,
I thought I could become
whatever I touched.

A year before, in another language,
I held the desert in my hand,
I tasted the iridescent sea.

Now I stayed quiet, afraid
I would never see it again, the sky
shattered into a million pieces
and falling around me.

I watched my mother inside
walking back and forth in her heavy coat,
and my sister rubbing her hands
to make some kind of spark.

I could imagine furnaces rumbling
all over America, heat rising
through the vents, parching the air.

And I stayed where I was,
someplace I had no name for,
not for the snow or my standing still
and watching it fall

beautiful wreckage
deepening
with hardly a sound.

IMMIGRATION TEST

Williamsport, Pennsylvania, 1963

My father was studying Spanish,
had two feverish weeks to learn it.

Soy un plato de comida, he was repeating
like a schoolboy from his notebook,
walking around the kitchen table,
"I am a plate of food,"
tripping over the chairs.

Someone had made an error,
told the authorities he knew
one more *lengua* than he did.

My mother was reading her cookbooks,
imagining the *vol-au-vent*, the *bouillabaisses*
she would never serve in America.

"I am a piece of sunlight," my father was saying,
yo soy un pedazo de sol,
"there is no darkness I cannot eat."

Our visas were hanging in the balance,
it was life and death, it was
getting it down or being sent back,
and my sister listening to the radio
knew big girls shouldn't cry.

Once, I found him in the cellar
writing on the whitewashed walls,
higo, granada, mango, fruits of his other life
that crossed idioms, hemispheres,
the dry orchards of Sinai, Sonora.

At the dinner table, no one could say a word
for fear of breaking the spell,
razing the strange house he'd been living in.

On the day he left for the big city,
I saw him under the full-leafed maple
reciting *Verde, que te quiero verde,*
as if he'd known it all his life,
as if he felt a green
more green now than any other.

The Book of Love

It was the Big Bopper on the radio singing
"Chantilly Lace" the wiggle in the walk
making me act so funny it was Louisa Richards
promising to play me her new clarinet
the reed softening in her pouty mouth
or even Miss Kelchner in her red pumps
tapping the globe with her fescue telling us
to follow the intricate map of our hearts
oh the world seemed suddenly round and flat
and many-sided who knew what was happening
how lost I was why Mr. Overdorff would slap
the back of my head was it for thinking
of Beth Reposo's ankles making her loafers
my favorite shoes for a month? *Look sharp*
he said *don't get too dreamy* but wasn't it
all a feverish surprise the dark of the body
like the dark of the moon mysterious oh to be
on that luckier side even Bill Corson flipping
the finger would throw me for a loop what
was it about symmetry that lured the eye
to the middle to the mouth the navel valleys between
and below that sent me scouring for meanings
words I knew by themselves but not like this
not almost touching each other *making out*
French kissing as if the secret were lying
in the thin elusive space in between
electric causing what new calibrations
what prayerful nights of wishing that maybe
it was only a sunrise away that someone
improbable would take my finger
and put it down in the book of love tell me
go ahead read it out loud even if several paragraphs
were missing even if all the pages were blank
and the story would have to be told
by heart as if I had written it.

High School Lesson

Jake Sims was to be paddled
because he hadn't known the names
of the three kinds of clouds,
no excuses.

In front of the class,
bent over and facing us:
three hard smacks
for cumulus, stratus, cirrus.

It was a long time ago,
though I'd like to know
whether he thinks of it sometimes,
Mr. Lawson looming over him,
telling him to brace himself.

What I remember most
is how red his face got,
red from pain, how he winced
as the paddle hit.

How many of us I wonder
wished he would cry out?

But he said nothing, sat down
and Mr. Lawson continued
as if something which had parted for a while
had now come back together.

It would be big news
in the hallway soon
and everyone was ready
for the bell to ring, maybe Jake
more than anyone else.

Already some of us were whispering,
getting the details right—

Mr. Lawson, for instance,
hanging his coat on a hook,
or Jake staring out
at our faces staring back,
or Mary Bell
putting her hand for a moment
lightly on his shoulder

and how no one budged then,
no one said anything for a while.

SOMETHING TO THINK ABOUT

Scientists have detected that the neutrino,
once thought to be massless, most likely has mass.
—Scientific American

It's the news of the day: neutrinos,
the ghostliest of particles,
are *something*, almost immeasurable,
though so many of them pulling together
might slow the expansion rate
of the universe.

It's similar to the parable
of the lion and the mouse,
how we shouldn't discount
even the smallest force.

And wouldn't I have been comforted
by this existential fact
the day Joe Barone
jammed me against the lockers
and said *You're a flea?*

Only Joe had never heard of neutrinos
and gave me the friction burns
on my scalp to prove it.

Which is why a liberal education
seems a fine idea, not only
for the smallest of us, but maybe for Joe, too,
who might one day find himself
needing a mortgage, say,
or standing in front of a hiring committee
of all his ex-tormented.

It happens, of course, in the ideal
version of our lives.

And what would be Joe's version?
That he keeps getting bigger?
Or not needing revenge because
who would be stupid enough
to cross him?

Or how one day, someone he's got
by the collar mentions something
like muons or neutrinos
because there's nothing else he can say
and Joe drops his hands
to feel some small part of the world
pass through him,
making a difference.

It sounds like *my* ideal version of his life,
though I'd like to think that sometimes
the ideal undoes its gossamer robe, dives
into the muck of our lagoon,
changing it for a moment.

Like the time Joe put his paw
on my shoulder and said, *You're okay*.

Which, of course, never happened,
though many times he walked by
without hitting me, or saying a word.

Free Love

1968

The decade was getting naked,
poets were singing the book of the body,
the times were unfurling

and we were unzipping our dresses
and pants, unhooking our bras, it was free
we thought, and maybe it was love,

no obligations, requitals,
because the revolution was coming
as surely as the riots had come,

the dark assassinations,
and looming around the corner
a one-way ticket to Saigon.

We were George and Abby,
Martha and Thomas, names as blue
as the blood that spawned them

but we were also Raul and Frankie,
Antoinette and Maria, all of us
making love, what better way

not to make war. We were taking
the pill and maybe the drugs, we were
trying to float above the cataclysms,

the history we heard
like a buzz telling us
not to repeat but make it new.

We thought we were seizing the day,
hellos, goodbyes, it was all the same,
every encounter erasing another,

and what we might have been doing
was maybe teaching the heart
the delinquency of our hands, our lips,

touching each other but almost
as though we had never met
and it would take years

for those of us who were lucky
to feel the body on our fingertips again
to say *love* and know the difficulty

of its being said, love free
maybe of any assurance, for as long as it lasted,
but love itself, without exemption.

THE FUTURE AS A NOTION
OF MOMENTARY PLEASURES

You are whispering *flame-throwers*
to the autumn leaves such swoons
of brilliant ruin over your roof even the car
you were driving last night along the dry
riverbed kept plunging into the liquid dark
creating the sound of water and don't you
suddenly remember why you were standing
under the streetlight for so long wasn't it
for its sheer incandescence it's what
you've been longing for the many small
enticements grass shoots brushing against
your ankles the moon lighting a pathway
through the neighbor's garden keeping the garden
indelible nothing spectacular one thing
and the next the anticipation of another
making you feel lucky to be anywhere a single
blue feather stuck in your shoe an open book
riffling its pages in your hallway now your neighbor
stopping by with stargazer lilies in her arms
hoping you'll like them you do it's what
you've been waiting for since that moment
she knocked and you opened the door.

III

Why I Have The Radio On

The family has gone off for a week
and I've stayed back to do
significant work which might crank
the century a couple of notches forward,
something with the wild odor
of the unsayable in it

and what I've done so far
is walk from room to room
remembering how a few hours ago
my daughter was chattering away
on the phone, and my son was listening
to some heavy metal delirium,

and wasn't it just this morning
that I sat with my wife on the porch
talking of solitude as balm for the soul?
Did I actually say *soul*
and could I have meant
something less imposing, like "nerves"?

What I'm trying to do
is resist the kitchen clock
which is ticking unforgivingly.
And the house has suddenly become
immense with too much light,
not a word I say will contain it.

So I make myself tea
and think of Li Po in his garden
unfolding the delicate lotus of his poems

but I'm also hungry
so I boil a hot dog till it's plump
like the ones at Coney Island
where I've never been

but I can imagine can't I?
while I assuage the animal in me
so it can burrow further
into the dark pocket of itself
to let me *think think think.*

But here's the mailman now
with letters . . . for everyone else—
so many unopened envelopes
accruing on the table with news
growing stale, news that might include
something irresistible, maybe about *me*!

So much to get done
and how is it that it's already evening
and time for a drink and the anchorman,
and maybe calling old friends

because it's hard
trying to get through the hours,
remembering the dog with its soulful eyes
and my son bobbing up and down,

and the world lying just around the corner
even with night coming on
and my own face staring at me now
from every darkened window.

WRITER'S BLOCK

Of course, there's always love,
or work, death or sex, these last two
intertwined sometimes like kudzu
in a Georgia field, and let's not set aside
the big N as in Nature, carrying the bulk
of poems on its diurnal back.

In a pinch, something surreal might do,
sheep in wolf's clothing, grass
that's greener on both sides, a candle
lit and burning at neither end,

though anything oddly domestic
will serve as well, a staircase
rising to nowhere but the ceiling,
clean laundry on a clothesline
billowing like seraphs, or bread crumbs
leading away from the garden gate.

Whatever you choose, the hope is
to begin with something open-ended,
some small parabola of thought
which might suddenly zoom you
in a gust of inspiration
upward on hoof and wing

where you might rarely travel
in your prim and Sunday clothes,
but from under whose sleeves
there might appear
in one epiphanous moment
the utter stranger
you have always been.

First Efforts

Always good to pick up so-and-so's first book
full of those wonderfully
inconsequential poems about napkin rings
and the meaning of animal husbandry.

And what about that immense
celebratory "Ode to Coffee," the spoon
in its cup *rising like a mast of insight*
from the dark unconscious.

Isn't it comforting to know
that the malarial cloud
of bad writing can linger anywhere?

Oh never mind the later work,
those brilliant, difficult volumes
that have elbowed their way
onto the narrow shelf of preëminence—

it's these first, trembling efforts
I'm after, fledglings in the palm,
larval stirrings which have yet
to test the steepness of flight.

And when the reading lamp
beacons our way like a star
from the deep socket of night,
I'm happy for having such a phrase
taking its turn in the vernacular of art,
awful as it is, especially
since it's not mine.

But it could have been.
And isn't it, after all, a sense of generosity
that makes one person try and fail
while the other looks on thickly from the wings,
wordless and too much himself?

So in my large chair I read
poem after struggling poem,
the heavy turn of each page
not quite metamorphosing into something
unthinkably feathery or muscular,

but giving me a notion of it,
a slight wind against my cheek,
an odor of something wild
ready to be unleashed from its constraints

like a hawk above, circling,
about to break deeply toward the pasture,
or a horse, suddenly untethered,
eyeing a long expanse of land.

TALKING TO MYSELF IN THE SHOWER

What fun to recite favorite lines here,
or even the newest recipe for stuffed squash,
the words reverberating in sheets of sound
against the tiles and tympanum.

I've managed to say the Gettysburg Address
in the time it's taken me to shampoo and rinse,
and could there be a better declamation
than the Boy Scout Law, ending as it does
on "clean and reverent," the temple
of the body upright for one more day?

And the conversations I've meant to have:
with the plumber, for instance, whose bills
have resembled Sumerian manuscripts,
indecipherable but for the numbers—
or the mechanic whose "special of the day"
has been to find everything wrong with my car,
his head shaking in sympathy as if to suggest
we are all as damaged as your gasket seals.

And the arguments I've never won—
how deeply satisfying to retrieve them,
drive them home again and again, revised,
refined in the alembic of my imagination
until they gleam.

And all the while, a steady drizzle of rain
on my shoulders, soothing pats on the back
as I stand naked before judge and jury,
both of whom, luckily, happen to be me.

But really, who doesn't long
for a second chance, getting out of the shower
with the fresh soapy odor of redemption,
the droplets of water crowning the head,

the old self, temporarily,
scrubbed down to the new:

now I catch myself in the mirror,
convinced I've never spoken as well
or looked any better than I do,
walking out into the grime

of the day's offenses, ready
for whatever else the world
will throw at me, or whatever
it has held behind, unfinished,
for me to come back to.

Mind | Body

How do they survive, riven
as they are, the one undoing
the other's desire?

Tell the body to outrun
the mind, and the mind smirks,
whispering too loudly
this way this way,
blocking all the exits.

And the body, luxurious
sensualist by poolside or in bed,
doesn't it hear the mind's
impatient machinery ticking
it's time it's time?

And only in our mind's eye,
as we're fond of saying,
someone else's body leaping nimbly
in *jetés* of thought, or revealing
to us Act V, scene iii
in one gestural flourish,
body and mind beautifully
synchronous.

Oh, the mind is eely, slipping
out of its puzzle boxes,
loving its own wit.

And the earnest body: speak of it
with the least irony, and already
you've begun to unnerve it.

Better to let them have their way,
forgetting about them both
until they meet again sometime
as if for the first time

in library or steam room
ready to shake *hello*

or lead you to whatever door there is
and always the two sets of stairs.

LOST POEMS

What happened to the poem I meant to write
whose first faint voice arrived
in the early evening when the stars
were about to glimmer "like so many jewels."

Easy to see why nothing came of it,
but the moment was real and the stars
were something *like* jewels and not
the ghost-eyes of the dead, or the slight pinpricks
of conscience, etc. Not even close.

And what about the poem whose words included
bestial and *vertiginous* and let's not forget *zippy*,
so many strange bedfellows, cramped
and elbowing each other on the floor.

And of course, always the poem
whose wild music swirled around me
like a bride's translucent veil
though the wedding never came off.

So many moments unpreserved
for want of luck or brilliance—
jazz riffs, great basketball shots,
the kiss of the century with Donna,
and even the minor occurrences
at the Hoagie Palace with Jeanine,
the way she said "Genoa" with pursed lips,
making me grateful for such a thing.

Like this moment at the kitchen table:
the daylilies outside the window
craning their orange heads toward the sun,
the white-throated sparrow
whistling its one-hit tune, just

part of the tableau this morning
though such a risk to mention it here
since *trill* might dangerously follow
and maybe *feathered messenger*,
and then the nasty problem of dew on the grass
looking very much now like jewels.

EMBARRASSMENT

It's the testimonial you give
at the retirement party
which ends on a poetic flourish—
It is Margaret you mourn for—
which seems suddenly, entirely wrong
for a bon voyage,
what were you thinking?

It's the worst move
at the father-son basketball game,
the clumsy blocking foul
on someone half your size.

Or it's in the p.p.s.
of the letter you've written her,
the joke about the dog
which repulses her forever.

What can you say of them,
such moments which stay with you
like the faintest music?

Or of these new ones about to arrive
like a hundred trumpets
blaring your wrong inflections?

"You've put on weight!" you blurt out,
meaning *you were too thin, you look terrific,*
"Your hair is such a gray," meaning
look at the lovely color you're haloed by
though all you've managed to do
is part the river of friendship,
drowning all good wishes in your wake.

Better not to speak, your other voice says,
better to sit with your hands in your lap

watching the perfect dancers swoop and turn
under the glinting chandelier.

And you do. Until life
in her evening dress
romps about you again
forgetting who you are,

forgiving you the stained tie
or the champagne glass
sticking out of your pocket

or the way you keep calling her
Marguerite, which she seems to like,
though it's not her name, or a name
she's ever been called.

THE GROOVE

Any athlete will tell you
it can't be bargained for,
though sometimes, you're one
miraculous rung below the paradise
you thought you'd never reach.

Even when you're mopping the floor
or raking the brilliant leaves,
you might be brilliant too, moving
as if you were all dance,
all Fred, and Ginger too.

And listen, you've been asked to speak
at the testimonial dinner, off the cuff,
but you're ok, you're in the groove
and the groove is doing all the talking,
one word licking the luscious next.

Isn't it time to crank up the tightropes
across Niagara, play your tenor riffs
on all the Bourbon Streets?

What a surprise to fall out of it then,
swinging at ghosts, tripping over
the least syllable, and here's a stranger
next to you at a backstreet bar
having a drink, tapping his fingers
in a way that shows you where it's gone

making him sound the way
you sounded months ago, if only
you could remember how it happened,

how you opened your door that day
and someone unexpected walked in
with an open ticket and a trunkful of clothes
and with no intention of staying.

ANXIETY OF INFLUENCE

The poem I've just written
includes a line so familiar
it's as if someone I used to know
were visiting from who knows where,
Paterson, Amherst, Rapallo?
taking lunch on the patio with me,
sleeping over for a few days.

I try to dredge up a face
from the banks of receding memory
but nothing snags.

"Who are you," I finally ask
after an embarrassing interval,
pulling out all the directories
when there's no answer,
scouring them like old photographs
or letters with a hint of perfume.

At night, I repeat a dozen names
hoping, dreamily, that someone
might peer out from behind a wood-pile
or a magazine in a waiting room.

Oh, whoever it is, I think,
how good just to have them near,
even in a house as small as this!

But soon it seems unbearable,
this putting up of a guest
who masquerades, now, as one of the family,
nudging an uncle out of his seat,
spooning out the last strawberry
from a cousin's pudding,
giving commands.

And, firmly, but with some
remorse, I ask it to leave,
helping it pack its bags,
the household a little unsettled,
the emptiness, emptier.

And as inscrutably as it arrived,
it disappears like something
that never was, leaving only
a space in the air
along the upstairs hallway
or at the parlor window

or even by the entrance gate
which has been left ajar in the wind
and is swinging wildly now
and clattering, and will not stop.

Against the Symbolism of Small Losses

So you've lost your keys,
your life's in ruin, over-
turning your simple afternoon.

Maybe it's the accrual
of all those other losses—
the stolen wallet, a shattered window,
the peach sweater stained
a deep cranberry red—
that's pushed you over the edge,
made you bleat your *woe is me*
to every neighbor.

What about your house? Intact.
The car: parked exquisitely
at your pleasant curbside.
Your dog: wagging a doggy tail.

But maybe you're thinking
in bigger terms, one *loss* leading
to all the others, first cousins
to the final disappearance
of everything you love.

Frankly, today, it's only made you
late for the movies, where your wife
has already found two seats together,
her head finding your easy shoulder

while a river of credits rolls along
and the music rises,
and the ticket stubs in your hand—
in spite of everything you know—
feel like crisp hundred dollar bills.

IV

BEGINNINGS

. . . innumerable adventures . . . and only the beginning.
—Jack Kerouac

The trees are so leafy this summer
we're breathing perpetually
under a green shade.

Every new moment is a door
that offers us the excitement
of unlatching it.

Now you come in from the garden,
the fluttery beginning
of the next instant.

I whisper another word into your hair,
it's not quite *another*, it's just one,
and one again, we're the giddy
amnesiacs of the present.

Outside, there's a sad old man
tapping his cane against the glass—
is it history again?—
looking at us with disapproval.

Such a lively bird perched on his head,
pecking at his nightcap, disheveling it.

What bad citizens of time we are
doomed to repeat ourselves
and we do, we do, every
recurrence the beginning
of just the beginning.

Here's a new window to turn to,
here's a cloth to clean the mists.

When you say my name
it sounds so momentary
I don't know where to turn.

ON A NATURE WALK IN THE SOUTHWEST DESERT

So many species to identify—
desert poppy, Swainson's Hawk—
my woozy brain reeling
in a whirlwind of precisions.

Soon, one petal blurs into another,
wings multiply into an ecstasy
of feathers, my memory
overwhelmed with eye stripes,
leaf serrations, lobes.

Indigo Bunting, the book says,
Blue Grosbeak, but I'm looking
only at the azure sky, thinking
this is what I'll take.

There's a movement in the mesquite
and I'm whispering "birds,"
there's a wavy hillock of color
and I'm seeing "flowers."

Now the sky is roiling
into a storm which, I'm sure,
has a name, but "storm" is just
what I want to call it,

as large a noun as I have
to account for every unexpected turn
maybe veering my way.

And isn't happiness unexpected too,
impalpable, floating lightly upwards
from the heart and lifting us with it?

There's my wife pointing at the Palomino,
calling it the yellow horse,
and I'm pointing back at her

thinking what a spectacular being she is,
all my words suddenly more ample,
refusing exactitudes.

"Honey," I say, looking at her red hair
and her low cut jeans, "*you're it*,"
and that makes her feel as extravagant
as anything else I've said today

the warm improbable rain falling now
over the whole expansive desert
making both of us think
of voluminous words like *capacious*
and *jubilation* each roomy enough
to contain everything brimming
around us, all we identify,
all we leave unnamed.

Love Poem with Crowbar

I've walked into the house, I'm trying
to put my finger on it. Maybe it's how
things have been reshuffled, the rugs,
the paintings that are playing musical chairs.

Maybe it's the sitting room suddenly
taking on the sharp scent of mesquite,
mesquite side table, mesquite credenza,
black pots on the shelves
with their large open mouths.

I can hear my wife on the back stairs
ripping the carpet up from the treads,
ringing the crowbar with her hammer
like an alarm, watch your step.

There's new wallpaper in the bedroom,
toucans perched in the broad-leaf vines,
lizards among the mangrove branches—
so many ways of looking at it.

It's as if she's rehearsing for some shift,
her small adjustments furthering us away
from the way we're used to.

On the news this morning, a cow
swept up by a tornado, found miles away
unharmed, nuzzling in the grass—
almost as if nothing had happened,
a small upsurge of terror,
then the taste of sweetness.

I don't stand in her way, especially
when her hands are too busy squaring her goggles
and all I can say is "Honey, unplug the Sawzall,
let's have some wine, feed the birds."

There are river stones on the sill
lined up like ellipses, horse sculptures
on the dresser that are made of straw.

Whatever proves too conclusive,
like this brick wall along the garden,
my wife sees in it the promise of a doorway,
the light slipping through.

Like the way she'll sleep tonight
with her face to the window,
the house quiet except
for her steady breathing,

what I'll be listening closely to,
hearing the river in it,
hearing horses at the edge
of the river, lithe and riderless.

OUTSIDE THE WINDOW IN JULY

They must be the Furies, these three crows,
making noise again in the early morning,
waging their outrage against the dawn.

Or maybe they're the Fates in dark habits
cawing the names of the saved
or the soon-to-be snipped.

Now they seem like reed-blowing pipers
squawking at each other in piercing tones,
repetition on a single note.

Charmed by their own cracked voices,
they clear the earways of any obstructions
these misfit singers in search of an ending,
poets who are all too epical.

Oh, you can curse and petition, pitch
your imaginary stones to heaven, but still,
they're there, shameless,
unremitting, loiterers who are in love
with more than the worm.

If only your room were windowless.
If the sedge were somehow withered
and no birds sang.

But soon, you find you're almost used to them,
your sense weaving a spell around their sound,
and in your deepest dreams
you hear them only as a chorus
of tiny sparrows on a wire.

Now you're waking up at a sensible hour
without the bedlam of those other days
you might remember with some wistfulness,

a time of raucous cries when
wake up wake up wake up
was as loud and adamant as any
advisory, your body alert,
your mind tuned to strange frequencies,
making such lavish connections.

Arizona Wind

Half the tin roof of the shed
is shifting back and forth
like a weather vane.

The birds are gusting away in mid-flight
and those ghost horses in the droughty field
have sent up dust funnels
that are drinking up the sky.

If there were a boulder on a chain
someone might bulldoze it
into the hardscrabble yard,
hook the house to it.

Yesterday, the moon for a moment
slid over the sun
and everything seemed under sentence.

Everything still is.
The dogs are chasing their own tails.
Widowmakers are groaning
their arias from every tree.

Hooray for the sun that will last
another billion years.
Dear gravity: save us now.
Mercy, lend us your coat.

The wind today is a woman with long hair
entangling all she loves.

Every rock is no heavier
than its weight in feathers.
A jewel may lie buried in each stone.

Whatever lifts has new wings.
Whatever sticks, sticks hard.

Conversation with Landscape

There may be moments when the world
    lies beyond any calibration,
like a word that's never been said,
   or a joy so private

not even the body can sense
    the small purl in the bone.
Sometimes an object falling faster out of the sky
  does so not for anything but love of the ground

and a woman pausing outside her door
    feels the completeness of grass, tree, stone
around the root of her standing,
   leans into it.

Sometimes another step is unnecessary
    to be where one is,
a conversation occurs
  without anyone's asking,

the wind arching through the trees,
    the river lapping at its dark alluvial edge—
the earth speaking to another earth
  inside us.

Whatever is strange is strange in its own language.
    Cup the wind to your ear,
the water in the palm of your hand.
   Something arrives that is not of our making

ONE AFTERNOON

We were on a screened-in summer porch
drinking beer and complaining that mosquitoes
had slipped in through the cracks,
the black flies were being pesky.

The thinnest wing beat,
the most trifling bit of blood on the arm
seemed consequential.

We couldn't know how some of us
had hearts timed to go off soon, tumors
that were already ringing a heavy bell.

Someone inside was singing off-key
and maybe we didn't mind listening to it.

There was a mushroom cloud forming
in a patch of sky, but it was just a cloud.

It felt almost pleasant to stay where we were
fooling ourselves and wanting to be fooled
in the golden afternoon light

and the daytime moon shining faintly beyond,
looking diaphanous, as if anyone
could see right through it.

ANIMAL DEATHS

Oh, it's stupid, I know, to be
so squeamish about every cruelty—
toads severed under mower blades,
deer gnarled by the side of the road—
when so many animals themselves
are too amply designed
for ripping tendon from bone.

Still, I wince every time I pass them—
pigs snuffling in troughs, steers
graining up in lots, doomed
to the abattoir and the butcher's hook.

Though better, perhaps, to have the bullet
to the brain than the cat's claw
pricking the body to exhaustion.
More merciful the sledge to the forehead
than the pack of mouths at the heel
slowly drawing a river of blood.

And here are the lobsters at the market,
crowded in a tank that seems insufficient,
a pot of boiling water steaming
in the back room where they'll end.

And yes, I've ordered two, happy
that someone else will cook them,
cowardly on my part, I know,
though better, perhaps, for the lobsters,
queasy as I am and clumsier for it.

Always some prayer to whisper
over the sweet white meat,
some blessing, too, for those
who bring such quick and sudden ends
as we might only dream of,

blessings to the python who snaps
the frail mouse in its love embrace,
to the lizard who tongues
the fly out of the air, blessed
the Great Horned Owl whose talons
are long and everlasting.

ARIZONA RANCH

My wife is standing by the Palomino
in her chaps and cowboy boots
holding the reins in her teeth
while she tightens the cinch.

She likes to ride, likes the feel
of a corral when it's crowded and dusty,
likes a horse to know what it's doing
when it's cutting cattle.

Yesterday, a Brahman bull
broke her arm against the squeeze chute,
turned it purple like the sky
that sometimes lours above the Chiricahuas.

There isn't much high ground for reproaching.
Out here, coyotes prey on the calves
still in their birthing sacs.
Out here, a steer goes to the boneyard
at the end of a chain and a pickup.

She'll be checking water troughs and pipes,
riding several hours around arroyos,
up stony ridges where the footing is tricky
and the fall is steeper than the climb.

Sometimes it's late when she comes home
and what look like houselights a mile away
are stars on the horizon, that kind of dark.

It's the fearlessness I like, or the way
she's open to the fear she has,
picking her way clear maybe to something
there're no words for, but it's there
in the land sloping away beyond fence lines,
subliming into larger silences.

It's hard country to live close to
without some luck and sure-footedness
and maybe the wind at your back.

She'll be gone most of the day
riding through snake grass and sacaton
closer to her life perhaps
for all that can take it away.

I'll be listening, later, for hoofbeats
on the pathway, whinnying from the barn
and the metal door clanging shut
that says the day has finally been unsaddled.

Until then, may lightning strike twice
wherever she isn't.
May she take the shortest distance
through bull pasture and thorn field.
May she find all the right gates
unlocked and swung wide.

V

Poem

So awkward when you start,
as if the body weren't made for it,
the ankles and vulnerable knees
ready to break apart against
the hard macadam or the whitest beach.

Even running on grass or dirt road
can seem unnatural, your feet chuffing
over a long grade, inscribing a record
of your wobbly progress, while the deep woods
on either side remain inscrutably quiet.

And the drama to your merest exertions:
calf cramps, back spasms and wrenchings,
the slightest twinge of the heart
giving you pause, like a comma,
by birch tree or hydrant.

Sometimes, of course, the body
might become another body,
retrieving its own rhythm and easing
briskly over several effortless miles:
how good it feels then,
as if you could go on forever!

Though always, if you've done it right,
the finish is difficult to imagine, your legs
beginning to grow leaden, pain
boring a hole in your solar plexus
and almost bringing you into confusion

but for the voice inside you
urging you on toward cemetery
or school yard or town square

where you never intended to arrive,
but here you are, flushed

with exhaustion and miles from home,
tipping your cap, saying *hello hello*
to the strangers looking your way.

CUTLASS SUPREME

My mother is 86, drives a Cutlass Supreme,
a vintage '72 hardtop orange coupe,
with a nose as long as a boat.

She likes the windows down,
likes peering over the wheel to see where she's going,
likes a couple of bourbons before dinner
to remember where she's been.

She names the twelve sons of Jacob
in French as fast as she can, *Ruben, Siméon, Lévi* . . .
counting them off on her fingers.
She says in Armenian, "The cucumbers
have all grown up and are hitting the gardener."
She says, *Se non è vero* . . .
"If it's not true, it's well conceived."

My children love to visit,
the dolmas, the lahmajouns,
and always poker after dinner,
how she's all in, and gives no quarter.

She's told my daughter, oh no,
not a doctor, the hours
are terrible, be a magician.
She's told my son, the guitar
is a lover's way to heaven.

I've seen her hula-hooping in the kitchen
while Dion crooned "Teenager in Love"
and the meat sauce bubbled over.
I've seen her twisting to Chubby "Checkers,"
he was so good, she wished him to be plural.

She likes Corneille, Hugo, she likes
not being a prisoner of words,
je ne suis pas prisonnier . . . but

aren't they all we have, and shouldn't we
rev them up, make them the best?

I bet she sometimes guns that V-8 engine,
backing out of the driveway, I bet
she sometimes whizzes past the market
and onto the open rush of highway
before she thinks of slowing down.

Let the road hogs beware, and those who think
that right is left, let them think twice.

My mother is 86 and reserves
the right to drive
wherever her turn signals take her.

PIANO LESSON

My teacher is looking at me sadly
as if with the large droopy eyes
of a Basset Hound.

I'm stumbling through "Naima"
transcribed for piano,
my fingers tripping badly over
the minor 3rds, the flat nines.

On his face, such longing,
as if it's the end of jazz,
we're saying farewell.

I'm ready to start from the top
playing all the changes, the repeats,
and he's holding his head in his hands,
swiveling slowly in his chair.

The song is full of smoke and aching,
like a woman in a shiny dress
walking through a dark hallway
haunting the man she's loved.

I can already feel the nostalgia in it
for what has never happened.

There are so many gray clouds here
I should play "Blue Skies,"
or "Mountain Greenery," their upswings
rising like colorful balloons.

Now I see my teacher lying on his couch,
cupping his forehead in his palm.
It must be raining in his heart
for a love of something so perfect
there's no place to find it

not in this room anyway
where I'm bent over the keys,
the rapturous jazz
just out of my reach

and my teacher is closing his eyes
and I'm closing mine
and we both might be imagining
Coltrane behind us breathing into his tenor

a song of love and departure
so fluent it feels like rain
falling into a lake

and maybe whatever is lovely
and improbable is always floating away
down a rivulet of dreams

where my body is falling
and my hands are reaching out,
and I am almost touching
something like water, like silk.

Nocturne

Standing in a field of corn on a still night
you know the sound of that field
by the rustle of leaf-growth and stalk.

You feel the course of a river
by hearing its voluble spillage over banks,
maybe by the feel of a witching wand dipping
toward an underground current.

The worm holds the earth in the length
of its body, and the bird attuning itself
hears the worm in the cave of its head.

So is your heart aware of its other heart
being among animals in the dark thickets,
moving within them as the scent
of the wild rose moves within the bee.

So does the stone dream of itself as a mountain
and the mountain of itself as a stone
and a man climbing a slope feels how his path
is both easy and difficult to manage.

Now while everything seems night-bordered
and still, the unseen coyotes of your sleep
are calling to each other across the valleys,

the hawk moth hovers at your mind's edge
with its nectared tongue, and in the midnight gardens,
the moonflowers have opened their white petals,
releasing themselves to the deepening sky.

SOMETHING CHANGING

That it might have been foolish
to fall in love with this world.
—Laura Kasischke

The man with the large biceps and tattoos:
pass him on a narrow street and you might
hold your breath, count your heartbeats.

But here he is, coming your way now,
following his Chihuahua on a leash,
the scale of the dog, the wawa in the name.

Sometimes I'm all for smaller things
like rat-dogs and butter knives
that turn the incendiary moment
into a fire by the hearth.

And those words that shout at us
from the public square—*hullaballoo,*
lollapalooza—say them softly to yourself
and you have Lola in her palace
hulling balloons without fanfare.

And maybe, once in a while,
if there's an elephant in the room,
that awkward silence among friends,
I'd like it to be a real elephant, thick
in the haunches, hiding nothing.

The birds are lining up along the wire
outside my window like a beaded necklace
singing on the world's shoulders.

In the quiet of winter, the trees
have put out roots at both ends,
roots in the ground, in the sky.

That man with the dog,
let's give him a dozen dahlias for his beloved,
and something in his pocket for the dog.

Sometimes the world can turn
upside down for the better, like this cake
I made for my wife and dropped on the floor
because, because . . . I was thinking

of the night of our first kiss
when we were barefoot and in love
with the ground, and the stars
were shining up at us from the river.

Night Traveling in Northern Vermont

Then the moose coming out of the pines
like a sudden dark glide,
a silhouette larger than his antlered self,
larger than the car or road

or the scent and density of the woods
he carried with him. I had to brake
and swerve to miss him
who'd held his right of way.

There was so much of him,
the world was moose for a hard
moment before he sublimed
into the adjoining dark.

Then the rest of the long drive
marking what was before, what was now,
as if something terrible and unholy
had suddenly passed through

without warning, making me want
to see it again and never to see it.
And the coming back to the house
with everything as I had left it,

the chair leaning idly
against the table, the teapot
on the windowsill,
the cut flowers still petal-wet.

And somewhere along the border,
a wildness traveled,
grunting across the marshland,
tonguing lily and pondweed,

so much of him of the earth
and most of him moose,
bog-heavy, gangly of limb,
long-snouted in the grass.

So Much of the World

So much of the world exists
without us

the mountain in its own steepness

the deer sliding
into the trees becoming
a darkness
in the woods' darkness.

So much of an open field
lies somewhere between the grass
and the dragonfly's drive and thrum

the seed and seedling,
the earth within.

But so much of it lies in someone
standing alone at the edge of a field
with a life apart

feeling for a moment
the plover's cry
on the tongue

the curve and plumb
of the apple bough
in limb and bone.

So much of it between
one thing and another,

days of invitation,
then of release and return.

SOMETHING ELSE

There's the lush grass again,
the white pines green and mysterious.
And the barn, too, in the distance,
fading red, the color of longing.

The afternoon light is gilding the hillside,
the clouds are moving together,
huge, incipient thoughts,

and you're swooning with desire
wanting the beautiful to lie down with you,
gold-leaf your fingertips and tongue,
green you with fragrance

though you don't know exactly
what you're after, whether it's beauty itself
or whatever lives inside it,
elusive, entire,
peripheral to your wanting—

shadow of wings
you catch obliquely
along the woods' edge,

river that you hear
without listening.

Recent titles in the Carnegie Mellon Poetry Series